Arrangements

Gabrielle
Journey
Jones

Also by Gabrielle Journey Jones

Spoken Medicine (2017)
Ginninderra Press

Etymology of Courage (2021)
Ginninderra Press

The Purpose of Truth (2023)
Ginninderra Press

Material & Ephemeral (2024) Co-Editor
Ampersand Duck

Gratitude

Deep gratitude, lifelong love and appreciation for my children Jai and Sofara, my family and community of friends. They encourage and inspire poetry, often without even knowing the joy they bring as we navigate the arrangements we make together in this captivating life.

To my mum, Patricia Jones, congratulations on your 80th birthday milestone and thank you for your love and support for myself, my siblings and your grandchildren. Now that you have a little more free time after 21 years on the Old Bega Hospital Land Managers Committee, thank you for proofreading this manuscript. I am also thankful for the editorial expertise of Katia Ariel, who provided professional feedback and consultation in a thoughtful and practical manner.

I am excited and grateful that my fourth collection Arrangements will join Spoken Medicine (2017), Etymology of Courage (2021) and The Purpose of Truth (2023) at Ginninderra Press. For all the times I have had to speak my own medicine, find courage and tell myself the truth, poetry has consistently been here for me. Much appreciation to Brenda Matthews and the late Stephen Matthews OAM for the opportunity and enthusiastic support to share my first 3 poetry collections with Ginninderra Press. It's wonderful to be part of the GP creative community, now led by Debbie Lee.

Special thanks to Ellen Van Neerven (EvN) for reviewing the first draft of this manuscript and inspiring me to complete it.

Acknowledgements
Poems published elsewhere

Aqua Nullius – earlier versions appear in Bega Valley Shire Council Talking Together podcast, 2023 and Ginninderra Press anthology *Telling Australia's Truth* (2024)

Local Gossip – an earlier version published in Pambula community anthology, 2023

Circular Breathing – Red Room Fellowship, 2024 online publication.

Arrangements
Print ISBN: 978-1-76109-712-6
Ebook ISBN: 978-1-76109-713-3
Copyright © text Gabrielle Journey Jones
Cover art: *Last Bouquet* watercolour painting by Julia Jacobs
Cover design: Graham Davidson
Typesetting Rack and Rune Publishing
Back cover photo: *Last Bouquet of Barrack Street*
Flowers arranged and photographed by Gabrielle Journey Jones

First published 2025 by
Ginninderra Press
PO Box 2 Bentleigh 3204
ginninderrapress.com.au

Overview

Gabrielle Journey Jones endeavours to balance busy life arrangements through the reflective process of a regular poetry practice. This collection is a sharing of her observations across many responsibilities including: managing a single-parent household with two gorgeous teenagers; full time Social Work at a regional hospital; a casual academic career; and running her own creative business, Poetic Percussion. Combined with precious time spent with loved ones, Gabrielle's work and social activities are a replenishing source of inspiration, joy and poetry. Self-care, meaningful friendships, community and family connections, and a passion for words are key themes throughout Gabrielle's fourth poetry collection Arrangements.

Contents

Acknowledgements of Country

Aqua Nullius	11
Looking Towards Thaua	13
Gulumada Windstorm	15

Social Arrangements

Local Gossip	19
Incandescent	22
Connecting Us	24
Shout Out To My Peeps	25
I'm Here	27
Oof!	28
Believe Me	30
Majority Said No	31
After SWIM	33
Mothers' Nature	34
Lifeline	35
Hospital Social Work Conversations	37
Poets and Social Workers	39

Family Arrangements

Chrysalis	43
Quiet Dog Night	44
Conversations with Time	46
Comforted	48
Sydney City Pride	49

Announcement	51
Homecoming	52
Last Bouquet of Barrack Street	53
Our Mum	54
Banksia Praemorsa	58
Collingwood Forever	60

Self-Care Arrangements

Self-Care Strategy	63
Source of Supply	64
Stuck	65
Phobias	66
Permissions	67
Press Pause	68
Loose Trolley	69
Pass the Parcel	70
Sleep-waking	72
Ballad of Self-Reflection	73
Today Tomorrow	74

Word Arrangements

Poetry Ponderance	77
Poet's Eye View	79
Telephone Messages	80
The Offering	81
The Journal	82
Template	83

Edit	85
The Quiet Ones	86
Set and Match	87
Varuna House	88
Circular Breathing	90
Alchemy	92
About Gabrielle Journey Jones	93

Acknowledgements of Country

This poetry collection was written on sovereign Aboriginal Land, Australia.
Predominantly on Djiringanj and Thaua Country, Yuin Nation.
Always was, always will be Aboriginal Land.

Aqua Nullius

Creek, river, lake, sea
Aqua nullius is a fallacy!
Creek, river, lake, sea
"No-one's water!!"
Said the British colony
Creek, river, lake, sea
Aqua nullius is a fallacy!

We can't erase the ways
Our waterways relate with us
We care and raise the ways
Our waterways connect with us

First Nation families
Custodial responsibilities
Caretaking waterways
Ocean farming respectfully
Aqua nullius is a fallacy!

Ancient knowledge honed
Women, men and children
Sixty thousand years
Of offshore technology
Aqua nullius is a fallacy!

Interconnecting ecologies
Flow from clouds, mountains
Hidden inlets to sacred beaches
Delicately woven on Yuin Country
Aqua nullius is a fallacy!

Communing with the moon
Travelling Thaua tides
Fishing this whale-road
Gathering eggs traditionally
Aqua nullius is a fallacy!

Casting strong salty nets wide
Sustenance for the whole tribe
Bountifully water provides
Balance, life and harmony
Aqua nullius is a fallacy!

Creek, river, lake, sea
Aqua nullius is a fallacy!

Looking Towards Thaua

Shapes off Bar Beach headland
Grey clouds in a leaden sky
Mountains in triplicate
Frame the long curve of
Oatmeal painted sand.

Tiny people far away
Sunbake, play and swim
The sea robed in turquoise
Lime and pastel green.

Couples stroll the lookout
Arm in arm before rain
Whispering to each other
Point at pelicans on Mitchies Jetty
And pack up picnic blankets.

The ocean is becoming choppy
Breaking waves splash foam
Across the emerald surface
In pairs too small for surfing.

The wind in a hurry brushes
Through eucalypt branches
Coastal saltbush and mangroves
Combing out seeds to be released
Along walking tracks and down the cliff.

A young cattle dog in a dingy floats by
Ears to the wind, tongue tasting freedom
Husband and wife dangle fishing lines
Hoping for flathead or salmon to take home.

Gulumada Windstorm

When the wild, sweeping
Deep salt water sea
Carved out these valleys
On Gundungurra and Dharug Lands
Two million years ago
It sculpted Three Sisters
A wondrous tourist destination
Cleaving to the edge of this gorge.

These fervent high winds
Mimic that ancient ocean roar
Boisterous breakers surfing treetops
Pushed into Katoomba from cliff drops
Barrelling into solid buildings
Varuna House is used to the noise.

Clanging window frames
Forcing open screen doors
Howling inside fireplaces
Wracking writer's last nerves
How the air bellows and screams!

Taunting games of disquiet
Discomfort and blustery unease
Ignoring the "Shhhh" sign
Planted near the entrance.

Rattling all the night through
Rolling in wave upon wave
Chaotic air currents careening
Crashing into poet's dreams
Full of emptiness and rage
This windstorm without rain.

Social Arrangements

Local Gossip

I heard a rumour in Narooma
How that tree hugger from Numbugga
Has the best bee garden North of Bega.

Honey sweet, dark and gooey
Farmed by a few of the sunburnt
Perma crew from Bermagui
You know who I mean?
Old mate Jake Hughes
They call him Hughie.

Hangs about with that flashy
Bold fella Beau of Bodalla's dairy scene
Acquainted through his Aunt Dorothy Brean
Their whole family blessed
With ebony curls and sun-kissed skin.

Beau and Hughie often gather up their music
And merrily road trip the valley together
Feeling grateful to see it so green.

They carpool (as they should) at Cobargo
Not far from the Wandella turnoff
Pack their instrumental cargo
Into Beau's shiny you-beaut new blue ute.

Hughie brings his marimba for Merimbula
He's a regular at the annual jazz festival.
Beau shreds his bass every other Saturday
With the Guitar Brah's in Tathra
Haven't made it out of the garage as yet
Everyone reckons they will.

Heading South, pit stop in Quaama
There's a predictable worn-out drama.
Beau does donuts beside the general store
He likes to show off a little just before
They take the bumpy unsealed back way
To visit another friend of Dorothy.

He's mostly broke but he's a generous, top bloke
Recently moved from Kalaru to Bemboka
The fabulous Charlie "Chuck" Roacker!
He sings lead and plays keys
A gifted emerging Liberace.

They jam reggae, disco and some country.
Eventually, all three mates get a hankering
For real coffee outdoors with community.

So Hughie, Chuck and Beau
Follow Buckajo Road to Candelo
It's definitely not the direct route
But it's Sunday and they are going slow.

They meander the monthly markets
Mingle with musos, yarn until the sun sets
As the creek flows again underneath Eden Street.
It's been four years since Black Summer fires
Crimsoned and cracked these innocent skies
Ripped savagely along Yuin songlines
Snatching up wildlife and human lives.

Scarring the hills from Timbillica
Right through Tantawangalo
Behind where Hughie, Chuck and Beau
Now prepare to drive the Princes Highway home.
Clear of ash confetti, hot embers, smoke and worry
They witness a spectacular view from Kanoona
A bright, white full moon rising over Djiringanj Country
Hoisted above Mumbulla Mountain like a beacon of safety.

Now that's a well-kept secret! All three mates agree
Let people gossip about the beauty they see
And everything achieved during bush fire recovery.

You see, they have been front line, first responders
No hesitation, volunteered with the Rural Fire Service
Co-wrote the Sapphire sound track of resilience
Still keeping watch in their own villages.

Hugging trees, saving bees, visiting those in need
Having a go at anything they hope will help most
They are heart, part and parcel of the Far South Coast
Our young men Hughie, Chuck and Beau.

We are glad to know local lads like them.
They're not larrikins, they are hurricanes
They storm right in when trouble begins
That's how we raise them here on Yuin Country.

* All characters in this poem are fictitious. They are representative of our amazing young people in the Bega Valley, NSW active during the Black Summer Border Fires 2019/2020.

Incandescent

For Wilfred Roach and Paul Capsis

Our conversations re-ignite seamlessly
Since we last gathered on Gadigal Land
Tonight, bursting with news we meet on Naarm
Cabaret mocktails, Dry My Tears, then late dinner.

Lightly dusted with "chocolate" soil
Mango mousse and coffee ice cream
To complete a delightful Peruvian meal
A special occasion with chosen family.

Boisterous laughter, deep gratitude
Appreciating this extraordinary couple
These men offer fireworks of enlightenment
By the love, art and integrity of their existence.

Celebrations whirlwind over a few hours
Collaborations, milestone achievements
Missed birthdays, readings, opening nights
Our podcast series launched courageously

Trailblazing black, queer writers
Podbean carrying All That We Perceive
An accumulation of shared wisdom
Worries, red flags, hopes and delights.

Manuscripts posted and contracts signed
Precious family reconnects into eldership
New ideas shared carefully, like kindling
Collected for future creative sparks.

Cheerful goodbyes hugged tight
Under Melbourne's gentle midnight rain
Nothing can dampen this rare blessing
The incandescent joy of friendship.

Connecting Us
For kitt

I know she feels me
Her portraits in ink and poetry
Loving up our small community
The joy on her face when she reads
Radiant as if gathering her words
From an overflowing well of happiness
She gets it, this gift of connectedness.

It is in the echo of the hollering ocean
She bottles in a video for her sisters
Sent from the most Northern tip
Of Big Island Hawaii, travelling
Across two active volcanoes
A sacred place to create.

She welcomes us into their home
We arrive instantly and sit with her now
Inside her kitchen through a camera lens
Sharing pots of tea with this week's poetry.

She invites us into their backyard
We wander their love-tendered tropical garden
Touch rain drops sprinkled on leaves
Enjoy her laughter close behind us.

Her hand on my shoulder as we walk
We can tell she's already sketching
The next few verses in her mind
Her eyes tracing our shapes
In swirls of black and white.

Shout Out To My Peeps

There's everyday friends
And now-and-then friends
Close and best friends
Precious and rare friends

Effortless friends
And no-effort friends
One-size-fits-all friends
One-of-a-kind friends

Trusted friends
And slippery friends
Super tricky friends
Short-term only friends

Emotional friends
Devotional friends
Beneficial friends
Unofficial friends

Seasonal friends
Reasonable friends
Toxic friends
Intoxicating friends

Huggable friends
Burst-a-bubble friends
No trouble friends
Board game friends

Ultra cool friends
Like poetry friends
Old school friends
University friends

Youth group friends
Fly-the-coup friends
Workplace friends
Social media friends

Single topic friends
Intellectual friends
Jealous friends
Rebellious friends

Take-a-bullet friends
Move-a-body friends
Soul family friends
Lifelong friends.

I'm Here

I'm here for comedy shows and laughter
I'm here for popcorn and happily-ever-after
I'm here for solid friendships over decades
I'm here for keeping each other's hearts safe.

I'm here for the bright green flags we wave
I'm here for the achievements we celebrate
I'm here for the road trips and holidays
I'm here for the corny poems and cliches.

I'm here for supporting the pathways our lives take
I'm here for drumming and singing beside seascapes
I'm here for sunshine, surviving cyclones and hurricanes
I'm here for all the blue in clear skies when they return again.

Oof!

Another
Everyday
Misculturing

And
Can I
Touch
Your Hair?

Just for a second?
It looks like steel wool!
You can touch mine

NO!!

I am not
What you think

Who you thought
Not to ask

What you
Assumed

That is not me!

It's all YOU

This is what
You need

Next time

Check
My
Biography

Before
You
Over
Reach

Reaching
Into
Me.

Believe Me

If I show you who I am
Will you believe me
Or still see me for who
You need me to be?

It's easy to breeze past
My lighthearted reality
I'm pleasing myself
Read my boundaries
Laid down, planted firmly
I seed them to grow
And hem me in safely.

I seek the same things
We all want for peace
And happiness on this planet
Spinning autonomously
In this strange galaxy
Of social expectations
And compulsory peopling.

If I show you who I am
Will you believe me
Or still see me for who
You need me to be?

Majority Said No

The chaos of "NO" echoes
Creates smoke screens
Obscuring our own truth
When the majority agree
Follow like lost sheep
Believe whatever lies
They are told to believe in
Only half listening
Doom scrolling
Any excuse, but if you tune in
Our silence right now
Is so LOUD
If we stand in solidarity
We can all quit pretending
We are not being used as weapons
Of mass concussion
Robbing First Nations equality!
Human rights decay
Resilience is stripped to grey
Parliamentary charades
Perpetuating pandemonium
Hoping activism fades
Leave this constitution broken
For future generations
Force them to rise up
Through our stagnant malaise
The oppressors always dictate
Deserving and non-deserving
Ignore how racism eradicates

This whole system breaks
Disintegrates over and over
White hands on the brakes
Blame dominant minorities
To keep us all in our place
Traditional Owners sidelined
What an international disgrace!

In Australia, on 14 October 2023, the majority of our country voted "No" to a First Nations voice to Parliament being added to our Constitution. Shame!

After SWIM
For EVN

"touch the wall, turn"
Backstroke in my belly
Breaststroke in my chest
Freestyle in my mind.

Their emancipated stories
Swim purposefully inside of me
Swirling, diving, up for air
Holding my breath
In wonderment and rage
Weeks after the pool closed
On that Carriageworks stage.

Bravely the protagonist
Asked us to safeguard
A breach of power
A drowning of trust
A torment of adolescent
Trauma memories amidst
Present day discernment.

Non-binary, not conforming
To change room door signs
Or prejudiced small minds
First Nations, queer, gender-fluidity
Reclaiming their spaces to flow
Connecting culture and humanity
Inside the healing ways of water.

Reflections on Ellen Van Neerven's groundbreaking debut play "SWIM", performed on Gadigal Land, Sydney 15 July 2024 at Carriageworks. Quote from SWIM (2024), introduced in Scene 12 LAP page 22.

Mothers' Nature

Triple Tree Goddesses
Float ghost-like across the lawn
Whispering incantations
Lichen-spun branches
Rising from their crowns
Moss eyebrows, moss cloaks
Sombre grey clay painted faces
Lips curled into expressions of kindness
Her magnifying glass invites
Closer examination
A watering pot so that we
Can show care and compassion
Lullaby of harp and bellbird
Encircles the dance
Triple Tree Goddesses
Swirl around the weeping willow
As cameras flash and videos roll
The message they carry
Embedded in their bodies
And also in ours: Save Her Soul.

Lifeline

13 11 14
You avoid Lifeline Australia.

13 11 14
You stare at this household number
On a faded blue and white fridge magnet.

13 11 14
You were encouraged by a friend years ago
The counsellors will help if you let them
They are professionals, available anytime.

13 11 14
You now know these digits by heart
But you have not felt right to call
You can not seem to justify it
You just stare at that old magnet.

13 11 14
You bravely save it into contacts
But do not press the green button
Fingers do not move to activate keypad.
You just stare, frozen at the silent
Static phone indicator icon, pleading.

13 11 14
You are numb, grieving, depleted
Yet other people must need it more
So many are worse off, you just stare
At an image on your screen lock
Taken on an unsuspecting brighter day
You still do not believe you should call.

13 11 14
You just stare, not wanting to tie up the line
In case someone else is struggling
And they can not get through
The operators would be too busy
For the indulgence of your trauma
You are socialised to rationalise
You always put other people first.

13 11 14
You do not want to survive like this
Overwhelm begins to coerce you
Into a familiar spiral of hopelessness
Places you have been before alone
You slowly stop staring, blink into your fear
Search through the contacts in your phone
Body tense, you nervously reach for a lifeline
At the tone, you press 1.

Hospital Social Work Conversations

Social Work is an interactive
Series of conversations
Consultations about plans
Worries and agreed actions
Integrated communications.

Social Workers don't always
Sound like the good guys
When we meet to discuss
Traumatic, stressful information
We are here for you to recover
Uncover, remember your truth
Important portals of strength
Within your current situation.

Only then can we begin
An open collaboration
Offer links to wider support
With your informed consent
Walking together
Mana kotahitanga
Māori language for the
Power of togetherness.

As we explore strategies
Starting where you are at
Mutual respect for your
Autonomy, not band-aid
Patronising promises
We listen to your requests
Because you are the expert
You know yourself best.

It takes time and can be difficult
To return to a place you feel
In control of your health and life
You don't want other people
Making decisions about you
Limiting your choices
You don't want to be told
What will happen next
From the sidelines
Of a hospital bed
Without a voice.

Social Workers
Advocate with you
For more options
We value your solutions
Government interventions
Are mostly voluntary
We require your permission.

Social Work is an interactive
Series of conversations
Thank you for your courage
Insight and participation.

Poets and Social Workers

We activate change with words.
We amplify expressed needs.
We give permission for feelings.
We bring community together.

We meet with respectful acceptance.
We advocate for social justice.
We nurture heartfelt story-telling
We celebrate marginalised voices.

We encourage self-awareness.
We tune into shared values.
We speak about our own healing.
We reach for self-compassion.

We craft communication skills.
We provide safe spaces to share.
We foster emotional well-being
We co-create messages of hope.

Family Arrangements

Chrysalis

Independence sneaks in
Like a caterpillar shedding skin
Primary school comes around
Separation anxiety begins.

Kindergarten whooshes by, next minute
High school enrolment papers are late
No more tears over maths homework
Time to test for learner driver plates.

Still somewhat a shock that my children
Can finally look me in the eye, standing
Hug me from on high with cheeky smiles
Develop compassion, become less demanding.

They hate to be told what they "already know!"
"Skibbity sigma, Mum! I got this, bro!"
My big little teenagers are transforming
Determining life routines on their own.

"Mum" becomes a background character
Called on for occasional goodnight stories
Friendship advice and city shopping trips
Long talks in the car on school holidays.

Emergent butterflies changing together
Awaiting adulthood in our family chrysalis
Anchored in the sharing of love and values
Looking forward to their metamorphosis.

Quiet Dog Night

My daughter's dog
Pats me on the back
With his soft white tail
A metronome of happiness.
He has climbed up on the lounge
Snuggled into the narrow space
Behind where I am perched
On the edge, marking papers.

His enthusiastic eyes peer out
He nuzzles under my arm
Busy, tiny chihuahua paws
Plump up the throw rug
He flops down beside me
Curls into a tan and white ball
Snores deeply while I work
My door opening duties on hold.

Too soon, he is wide awake, yawning
Stretches his whole body, then shakes
Leaps onto the plush floor rug
Plonks himself on my feet
Blinking into the warm air
That pumps rhythmically
From the small fan heater
Enjoying being front row.

My son barrels into the kitchen, hungry again
Dog shoots over to him like a wobbly arrow
Scrambling across the wooden floor
Hoping for a treat, no luck!
Just a quick cuddle before the pup
Leaps back up on the lounge
Breathing over my right shoulder
I take a selfie to send my daughter.

School holidays are strange times
For pets when their person is away
Confusion when 3:30pm passes quietly
He does not hear her key open the door
Inviting him into their special routine
Still, he listens hopeful for her return
Familiar footsteps, hugs, big belly rubs
It's two years today since he adopted us.

Conversations with Time

Conversations I am having with Time
Are becoming easier after half a century.
Sydney's Crown Street Women's Hospital
Chubby newborn hands holding Time close
Like a soft teddy bear full of wonder and warmth
In that forgotten Gadigal forced adoption ward.

Raised on sovereign Ngunnawal Country
Twenty-one Summers in our Bush Capital
Time granted a nurturing, unhurried childhood
Barely a whispered word from Time
Until our old tabby cat Tiger died graciously
Time attended the funeral we conducted
And I started to regard her more suspiciously.

Time has been a compulsive thief
She has stolen uncountable loved ones
Whisked them away without warning
In a fancy black and gold convertible
Vanishing precious people beyond
Forgiveness to somewhere irreversible
Weaving loss into patchwork amnesia.

Winter Time arrived late last week
Bitter breath tearing off Autumn leaves
Stripping branches along main streets
Frosted flowers on icy grass-lined paths
Seasons change as the calendar rotates.
Time employs clever, unsuspecting ways
To finalise closing chapters of our biographies
And the next generation that we create
Grieve as they are made to claim their place.

Time knows how my ageing body groans
Deep in these aching joints and thinning bones.
I woke up this morning in a cold room
Thankfully not dreaming of deceased cats
Chasing me around New York City
Begging with a multitude of meaows
To join me here for fresh country air
As Marge Piercy once experienced, while sleeping.

My life is in Australia, 16,500 kilometres
As the sulphur-crested cockatoo flys
From Wellfleet Massachusetts
Piercy's abode of dreams and poetry
Now I read her words as they travel though Time
Inside my ice-cold weatherboard house
Which has been home to local farmers
Their families and noisy feline ghosts
In the Bega Valley since 1935
Those who inevitably finished
Their conversations with Time.
It is a strange, steadfast comfort
That I will be no different.

Inspired by the idea of Cavorting with Time, Jacqui Malins (2018). Ref "I awoke with the room cold" in Living in the Open, Marge Piercy (1976).

Comforted

I fall asleep reading, comforted.

Marge Piercy's words
Follow me into dreaming
Her collection closes over my hand.

Contentment in Peace Cottage
As wintry weather invites itself in
An unwanted guest at the windows.

Surrounded by poetry books
Comforted by other people's
Thoughts and reflections.

Antique white, freshly painted walls
Old-style picture rails turn
Every room into a private gallery.

A treasured artwork watches over me
Twin elder tree branches gently meet
Catching poems on silver leaves.

Two bedside lights: one for reading
One for warding off nightmares
And imaginary burglars.

A favourite ceramic rainbow mug
Traces of orange juice, no vodka required
Never acquired the taste.

Sunflowers wide open seek the sun
Screen printed on my doona cover
Electric blanket on medium.

I fall asleep reading, comforted.

Sydney City Pride

My birth city
First home town
Returning to study
In my 20's city.

My pains-taking city
Career-making
Identity-shaping
Heart-breaking city.

My children's city
Family connections
Creative adventures
Life-long friends city.

Deep gratitude for my city
Travelling half a century
Down these memory lanes
And familiar Sydney streets.

I have always been a visitor
In my city, on Gadigal Land
This is where my people march
Together in Rainbow Pride
Courage and celebration.

A wistful gaze of hope
At the starting line
A 50-minute dance
Acceptance, existence
Resilience, resistance!

Glitter smiles in Taylor Square
The eyes of the world on my city
Twinkling back at us with love
Like a million stars borrowed
From the Southern Cross.

Announcement

Safer Travels Railway
Final announcement:

Reminder to all passengers
In rows G, A, B and E

You do not need to alight
Here at Toxic People station

You deserve better destinations
You burnt your own passport

To visit unsafe places
This stop is not an option

If you attempt to step off
You will, as you have requested

Be detained on this train
By concerned family and friends

Until we depart this station
Please return to your seat.

Homecoming

Suburban houses stretch for hours
Along streets with lights so powerful
The stars are hidden permanently

Perpetual midday vanquishing night
I used to live here, in younger days
Lost in concrete towers for decades

I relocated in search of better views
Unpolluted sparkles of the Milky Way
My family and I, we choose to stay

7-hour drive from our birth place
To the land of the Djiringanj
Until time brings change

Stark contrast, metropolis and country
Our daily lives blessed abundantly
Yet I still yearn a proper belonging

Ancestral lands, Africa and Pacifica
Where is my family sky, sea and mountain?
Gaia whispers homecoming through my veins.

Last Bouquet of Barrack Street

For my children, who lived here once and my parents who planted roses.

It's closing night, bittersweet sorrow
Gladioli grandiflorus sunshine yellow
The backbone and raison d'etre
Simply to shine and hold its own.

Strong fragrance of Double Delight
Front and centre puffed out proudly pouting
Stunning worlds of beauty in red and white
Unchallenged amidst this quirky bunch.

A shy General Gallieni quietly retires
Ruby red glow overshadowed on all sides
Pressed in by roses much larger in size
Still, a sense of timelessness abides.

Just Joey leaning as if seeking the sun
Pretty apricot petals humbly displayed
Waving frills share a spicy intense fragrance
Obvious choice voted as a world favourite.

Adorned in dark deep velvet red blooms
Black Madonna atop this final arrangement
Centrepiece of Mum and Dad's quarter-century
Carefully tendered Barrack Street rose garden.

The Last Bouquet of Barrack Street photograph and arrangement (as described above) by Gabrielle Journey Jones and watercolour impression "Last Bouquet" painted by Julia Jacobs appear on the covers of this collection, Arrangements.

Our Mum

For Patricia Jones

Nurse Robinson's Private Hospital
On a cold Wednesday, June 1944
In a busy brown brick Arncliffe house
Our Mum Patricia Enid Clay was born.
Enid and Lionel had been married 18 years
Their eldest, a young man already raised
Patricia grew up a helpful middle child
Her baby sister joined them in 1948.

Other famous people born in 1944
Alice Walker, Diana Ross, Gladys Knight
Bob Brown, Paul Keating, Peter Allen
Peter Harvey and Ray Martin
Our Mum grew up amidst this cohort
Baby Boomers shaping the world
Telling their stories, singing their songs
Emerging from the impact of raging wars.

Political unrest, global protests
Civil Rights, Women's Rights
A generation of fight and flight
Our Mum taught us to stand up
Against racism and ignorance
Through the 1970's and 80's
Instilled in us lifelong strategies
For happiness and self-confidence.

Celebrating eighty years in 2024
Our Mum is no frail little old lady
Although ageing bodies demand a price
She has survived the surgeon's knife
More than twenty times since 1975
Cancer, cataracts, a new hip, skull stitches
Countless needles in her eyes, arthritis
Swollen legs and significant hearing loss.

Our Mum is an ageing undercover agent
We have rarely heard her complain
Most days she simply lives with pain.
Quietly gets the job done, whatever her body asks
She ensures her medical team are up for the task
Wonder Woman from down under
Role model, leader and advocate
A Super Mum with a courageous heart.

Our dear Dad died, September 2019
52 years Alan Jones besotted by his wife
Our Mum's best friend, soul mate, true love
They first saw each other across the office
Child Welfare Branch, Darlinghurst 1966
Meeting after Mum graduated Bachelor of Arts
Our Mum in her first job as a case worker
Our Dad as a fledgling psychologist.

Within 12 months their families gathered
At the Methodist Church in Beverly Hills
Following their wedding vows they drove North
Dad's car almost did not make the long trip
To honeymoon at far away Kingscliff
After many tearful, discouraging years
Doctors determined our parents infertile
Our Mum would never carry their own child.

1973, they moved to Canberra from Sydney
Lovingly raised four adopted children
Each from mixed cultural backgrounds
Our Mum and Dad gifted us unconditional caring
An ocean of laughter and full-hearted kindness
A safe home, patient parenting and sage guidance
Shared values, generosity, family council sessions
To air our grievances and acknowledge achievements.

Throughout her career our Mum listened
Tuned into what clients expressed and needed
She was resourceful and community-minded
Retiring in 2000 from a career in human services
Built on skills, compassion and common sense
Our Mum knew how best to help people in crisis
Keeping well-measured and calm under pressure
She is still there for us, willing to share great advice.

Our Mum's gardens were a welcoming place to be
In both family homes at Bridge Place then Barrack Street.
To wander the plethora of sweet aromas grown so tenderly
Is witness to the same nurturing she has shown us consistently
Over 80 years, we are recipients of an intergenerational gift
Our Mum's childhood, her parent's values, love and resilience
For some benevolent universal roulette spin of incredible luck
We have been blessed abundantly with our adoptive, real Mum.

Banksia Praemorsa

For Alan Jones

Growing up, banksia bushes
Looked angry to me, spiky and rough
Hardy, webbed all-weather leaves
Attractive to birds, dangerous to touch.
But their burst of bright yellow flowers
From each woody spike felt soft
And fascinating, like mini corn cobs
The makings of Big Bad Banksia Men
Whom we knew well and feared a little
Villains of May Gibbs' gumnut stories.
My parents planted Banksia Praemorsa
27 years ago in their front garden
Lining the paved path to the garage
Flowering gargoyles of native variety
Overseeing all the activity of Barrack Street.

One day, there was an ambulance in the driveway
Mum rang to say Dad had forgotten how to walk
His legs gave up after getting out of the car
He had slid gently down onto the path in her arms
And was lying under the Banksia bush
Protected by a thick canopy of sharp leaves.
I wonder what my Dad was thinking
As he looked up into the grey Spring sky
Through the flowers he had nurtured
On that garden path he had paved
Decades ago before his mind began to fade
This property was their retirement paradise
And the last time Dad would see his home
All he wanted was his morning routine
A cup of tea at the dining table with Mum.

Instead, Mum and I gulped a quick lunch
Gathered Dad's clothes, glasses and toiletries
Raced over to South East Regional Hospital
Met up with Dad in the Emergency Department
Where he was being triaged compassionately
We hoped there would be a few tests
Before we could take Dad back home
Ten days later in palliative care, he was gone.
After struggling with pneumonia for a week
Dad had slipped into a bronchial deep sleep
Morphine to manage pain and help him dream
We stayed beside him day and night
Family arriving to hold his hand, say goodbye
Retelling stories, reading poems, video calls
They were the most precious ten days for us all.

Dad's farewell service was held on the green lawns
Of Old Bega Hospital, an historic place to say goodbye
We waited two months to try and let our grief subside
The weather matched our hopes for a bright blue sky
Just like dad's ever-curious childhood eyes
The platinum blond oldest brother of four
Sydney boy, soldier turned clinical psychologist
Dad was a planner, he would have been proud
We did not rush preparations, family had to fly in
On the day of Dad's funeral we gathered offerings
To celebrate his life with decorations freshly chosen
From the Australian native garden our parents created
I cut the flowers carefully, ensured we had a good range
His two grand-daughters carried the stunning bouquet
In the centre, beamed smiling faces of yellow banksia men.

Collingwood Forever

For Wayne Gillingham (RIP)

The Mighty Magpies, made Premiers of 2023
Champions of the Australian Football League
Defeated Brisbane Lions, four points in the lead
Upholding good old Collingwood's proud name
Considered one of the greatest AFL grand final games.

Five days before the Premiership Cup was claimed
The Magpie Army lost Sergeant Major Wayne
We hoped that he had found a comfortable space
To watch that winning end of season battle played
Maybe he even had a hand in tipping it their way.

Family and friends gathered from far away places
Shared favourite stories from Wayne's five decades
We wore "Collingwood 1892" club pins engraved
Buddy, their golden retriever, sat quietly centre stage
Beneath Wayne's casket, Magpie logo decorated.

Wayne and Buddy were besties right from the start
We miss them both, passing just ten brief months apart
A new cycle of sadness, as we hold them in our hearts
They are inseparable now, watching over my nephews and sister
A legacy of love united in family and "Collingwood forever".

Self-Care Arrangements

Self-Care Strategy

Poetry is my self-care strategy
Expression of what's messing
With my soul, needs to be free
All "Truth will out"eventually
Society begs please hide unpleasantries
Do not spill the tea on reality.

Isolation is waiting if we do not speak
We face instant consequences
When we lose touch with integrity
Closeting trauma quietly
Chronically editing our stories
Shame spirals beget misery.

Poets pin hearts on our sleeves
A problem shared is halved
S i m u l t a n e o u s l y
These little cliches matter to me
Words have saved lives once or twice
Including mine, to write is a relief.

I pick up my power pen on the daily
Let every feeling flower subjectively
Open for the sun, self-compassionately
It is not flattery if I respond poetically
To people and places surrounding me
Poetry is my self-care strategy.

Source of Supply

I am a source of validation
Appreciation and admiration

I am a resource of capitalism
Non-consenting exoticism

I am a cause of confusion
Misculturing and exclusion

I am a course of medication
Antibiotics for bacterial narcissism

I am a force of feminism
Fierce intersectional activism

I am a choice of determinism
Inevitability and individualism

I am a chain of reaction
Habitual truth-telling on repetition

I am a grain of underestimation
Manipulators downplay my observations

I am a game of backgammon
Chance, luck, skill and intuition

I am a flame of indignation
Righteous anger overcoming oppression.

Stuck

Suppressing
Expression
Mind hiding
Body knowledge
Disconnection
Left guessing
Digressing
Experiencing
Indigestion
Reflections
Seeking
Reconnection
Breathing
Emotions weaving
Traces of believing
Must be more than this
Perceiving paths of bliss
Neurospicy promises
Anonymous tips
Received in parenthesis
Find a quick fix
Shake loose
Unstick

Phobias

A fear of heights
The fear of falling
A fear of water
The fear of drowning.

A fear of fire
The fear of burning
A fear of queer
The fear of turning.

A fear of dogs
The fear of biting
A fear of friends
The fear of fighting.

A fear of love
The fear of losing
A fear of freedom
The fear of choosing.

Permissions

Permission to not know the goal
Permission to abstain from identifying the goal
Permission to offer no explanation for being without a goal
Permission to feel completely aimless for five freaking minutes
Permission to enjoy the natural happiness of making art for oneself
Permission to bring all aspects of oneself into poetic expression
Permission to play art and crafts in the company of friends
Permission to plan and attend solo creative missions
Permission to review my permissions anytime
Permission to take a break from creativity
Permission to not know the goal.

Press Pause

I envision my arm reaching around to collect
And connect my seat belt buckle three times
Before it happens, while staring blankly ahead
At a stranger in her red mini van filled with children
Also appearing to summon the will to drive home.

It is 7:05pm in the supermarket car park
Friday night at the end of one hell of a week
Counting women's dead bodies at work
Feeling these losses numb my nervous system
Poured like hot tar underneath us in the bitumen.

I hold the disenchanted gaze of mini van Mum
Both of us staring at tough memories on replay
Until I finally hear my belt click into place
Slide the black sash firmly under my arm
Only a few seconds have actually passed.

I breathe out, determined to leave
I breathe in the familiar warm aroma
Thai takeaway waiting on back seat
My kids will be ready for dinner
Unpause! I start the ignition.

Loose Trolley

"She's always by herself, always."
The customer service staff
Use telepathy to communicate
Which she intercepts reading
Their kindly concerned faces.

However she rejoices in the quietude
The silence to shop, think and reflect
In solitude, everyone around her is busy
Her kids don't go with her anymore
Independent, they are half way grown.

She notices a hastily discarded
Shopping trolley under the floodlights
No rush to rejoin the captive pack
Not ready to work or be jammed
Cramped in those short chains again.

The supermarket is closing
Staff emerge and draw together
All of the eloping trolleys
And they are danced across
The yellow-striped concrete.

They seem to catch on dips and cracks
As if they had enjoyed their break
There is still one loose trolley by itself
Loitering under the carpark lights
Forgotten and now free for the night.

Someone will fetch and connect it
But for now it is perfectly alright
To remain here quietly, alone.

Pass the Parcel

As the music of life pauses occasionally
What is wrapped inside the black and white
Stories we tell ourselves about loneliness?

First layer of recycled newspaper
Peels and reveals a deep sense of relief
Second layer a chocolate frog

Third layer unveils the beauty of spaciousness
Fourth layer, a pack of mini colouring pencils
Fifth layer, childhood memories of time out and solitude

Sixth and seventh layers accidentally rip off together
A sheet of African savanna animal stickers and
Poor advice on the inherent safety of avoidance

Eighth layer is tough, too much sticky tape
A "get out of toxic friendship gaol" free card
Ninth layer, a strawberry cream lollipop

Tenth layer, a cryptic quote: "Loneliness is not what you think "
Eleventh layer, a green plastic whistle for anything that hurts
Twelfth layer, a lengthy list of expectations for extroverts

Thirteenth and final layer a small cardboard box
Rattles when shaken, sound of a ticking bomb
"This is your wake up call" written in bold, red letters

Inside, an alarm clock and taped to its glassy face
A powerful permission slip to unwrap
One of life's most under-rated treasures:

An invitation to make time befriending loneliness
She is a lone lioness, strong and protective
To appreciate her presence is a rare privilege.

Sleep-waking

Am I dreaming the lives of people
Who once slept on this hotel bed?
Am I glimpsing how it feels to be them?
To struggle for freedom, flee harm
"Pack what you can in a garbage bag
And run, my dear cousin, run".

To fall in love with the wrong person
Watch them drive away twice
With my disintegrating heart
In a fancy, silent electric car
To play golf in a storm and be hunted
Sprinting along endless empty roads.

Crossing hazardous waters in pirate ships
To experience things I've never done
Layer upon layer of restless dreams
Wake, sleep, each time return more deeply
To strange landscapes beyond my reality
And faces of people I have never seen.

The haunting stories they tell me, I listen
Observing, attentive, seeking meaning
I wonder if stirring is still sleeping
These wild scenes inspire me, whispering
Enjoying this thin veil between worlds
I lean in: dreaming, drifting, sleep-waking.

Ballad of Self-Reflection

Wondering who I am, remembering
What change it has taken to become
The woman in the mirror standing
In front of me with all I've overcome.

Choosing myself is a rare opportunity
To reflect on life's smorgasbord
Friends float in, staying or leaving
I am inspired by their unique voices.

Impressions, experiences, out breath
Half a century tasting limitlessness
Unassuming, my changing isn't done yet
Reinventing myself feels like progress.

I never want to reach a static point
Where I stop questioning who I am
Self-compassion is an oil to anoint
My temple with every self-reflection.

Today Tomorrow

We all have this
Same moment
Right now:
Today.

We may waste
The offer by
Looking back or
Wishing forward.

We all want for
Something better

Finding contentment
Seems a life sentence.

We all want to make art
That creates difference
Personal and permanent.

We all witness
The present
Listen:
Tomorrow

Is happening
Right now.

Yesterday's dreams
Are today's
Self-care
Plans.

Word Arrangements

Poetry Ponderance

I invited a question
To fully form
How would I feel
Without poetry?
Might I become
A better writer
If I stopped
For a while?
What if I choose to end
Hiding behind words
Attempt to feel my life
Uninterpreted by pen?

Let the words
Circle my body
A little longer
Before catching
Feelings inside
A line or a verse
Let them move
Let them land
And move again
Let them go
Without the urge
To write them down.

Curious analysis
Emotional paralysis
It's OK to feel
And then forget
It's OK to heal
And still regret
It's OK to love
And then reset
Body knowledge
Will guide us if we let
Intuition ride shotgun
Beside our intellect.

Ahhh another poem
Processing emotions
Documenting my response
Repairing dissonance
Pride or nonchalance?
I write because I've learnt
Beyond certainty, for once
Allow myself to be ensconced
Poetry is a perfect ponderance
I must follow this enchantment
Meet my words for a one-on-one
To truly feel what my heart wants.

Poet's Eye View

Adjust expectations
A just expectation?
Many of us exist
On modern-day
Southern plantations
There are slaves
In the house
Slaves in the field
Our DNA filled
With racism's guilt.

Society fuelled
By bullies in pure silk
STOP the kill or be killed
Shield love that heals
Adjacent they build
Excuses they wield
Excuse me I will
Speak what I feel
I'm keeping it real
Like the poets I view.

Telephone Messages

To Poetry
Release my fears
Speak my truth.

To Music
Dance my grief
Soothe my heart.

To Art
Spark my colours
Fill my joy.

To Creativity
Heal my sorrow
Celebrate humanity.

The Offering

I read a poem
And could not
Understand
What it meant.

I stopped trying
To figure it out
Decided to just
Let the words in.

The imagery
Exquisite paintings
Like none that
I had ever seen.

The poetry
Little photos
Of places
I had never been.

The ways my mind
Set about opening
When I stayed present
To the offering

Of poems not taken.

The Journal

All the words tumble
Stirred with glossy paint
And the household names
Of modern Australian poets.

Award-winning verses jostle
For priority in the contents section
Stories in this high art magazine
Crowd and uncrowd these pages.

A dissymmetry of patterned letters
Both strange and familiar concepts
Jumble about as I try to make sense
Foreign to my understanding of genre.

Shape poems awkwardly self-reflecting
On the validity of their form and existence
Showcased within this curious periodical
Words selected and vetted quarterly.

Snap! I shut the publication quickly
Sensory overload sparks new thinking
Unconventional ideas I can begin
To visualise eventually revisiting.

Template

Front cover
Colophon
Copyright
Author
Artwork
Publisher
Printer
Previous work
Title page
Dedication
Contents
Foreword
Blank page

Chapter title
Epigraph
Graphics
P
O
E
T
R
Y

Chapter title
Epigraph
Graphics
P
O
E
T
R
Y

Chapter title
Epigraph
Graphics
P
O
E
T
R
Y

Post script
Author biography
Back cover.

Edit

Slash, cull, burn
What remains?
What returns to the realm
Before words were written?

Before precognition
Before sensations
Before feelings
Before permission

Before thoughts
Imprinted memory
Before healing
Reached the body

Before breathing
Before reason
Before waking
Before dreaming

Slash, cull, burn
What remains?
What returns to the realm
Before words were written?

The Quiet Ones

Some poems
Don't want to be memorised
They do not want to ever be
Called upon haphazardly
They do not wish to be noticed.

Some poems
Like to keep to themselves
They prefer a pristine quiet nook
Inside a tightly closed book
High up on dusty shelves.

Some poems
Have difficult stories to tell
They believe it is safer
Not to open up sad spaces
They protect us and mean well.

Some poems
Do not fully understand
They hold healing powers
Within their lines and verses
Wisdom of a life examined.

Set and Match

A scrunched up set list
Pulled from my pocket
Smoothed out, tucked under
A trusty microphone stand.

Thick red marker pen edits
A rite of passage for poets
Singer-songwriters and live bands
Keepsakes later saved in scrap books.

A set list is not to be written
In tiny letters on a post-it note
The words have to be big enough
To read from on high, without glasses.

I need to write a large set list
For my final gig before hiatus
A spontaneous and long awaited rest
Quality family time, not performances.

Holding poems in my frontal cortex
I already miss meeting them there
Poetic photographs of experiences
Political statements fighting systems.

It will be difficult to stay away, somehow
From communities of the spoken word stage
A grieving process after three decades
It's game, set list and match, for now.

Varuna House

Writers share common spaces
A literary lounge and sunny offices
Framed by a delightful spectacle
Hundreds of printed word collectables
The satisfying smell of books to motivate
We wake early, create all day.

Commune at dinner time
A feast arrives by 6:15pm
Enjoy adult conversations
Encourage each other
Laugh and compare
Our unique life stories.

Collaborate on clean up
Type away late into dreaming
Quietly a week slips by
50 solid hours spent on
Uninterrupted creativity
A most extraordinary gift.

Themed rooms are ready
For work and deep rest
Comfy bed, ample desk
Enough cupboard space
For clothes to relax
Surfaces for personal effects.

A bedside lamp
Tall bookshelves
Full of familiar names
Tempting to read all day
I brought some company
A lucky bamboo plant.

Sits on my desk
Three green shoots
Representing my family
Helps keep my focus
On growing and tending
Life experience as poetry.

When the window
Starts to let light in
Warming the carpet
And the day yawns
"Good morning, I'm here"
My game plan reappears.

Creative goals from yesterday
Must be adhered
Make the most
Of this spaciousness
Time must not be squandered

A conscious concise regime
For word flow is followed
Shower, breakfast, brush teeth
Rush back into routine
Begin where I left off last night
And write, poet, write.

Circular Breathing

Breathe in truth.
Simultaneously
Breathe out loss.

You hear poems
Being moved
Through you
How they resonate.

Words activate your chakra
Captivating imagery cascades
Free fall from the top of your crown
Imprinting throat, heart and solar plexus
Softly grounding in your muladhara.

Breathe in truth.
Simultaneously
Breathe out loss.

You feel poems
Being moved
Through you
How they medicate.

Intravenous lines injected
Poetic antibiotics ingested
For a soul in sorrow's descent
Inspiring your shaking pen
To administer healing rhymes.

Breathe in truth.
Simultaneously
Breathe out loss.

You lose poems
Being moved
Through you
How they dissipate.

Truth-induced amnesia
Forgetting most of the bright
Fluorescent isotonic words pumping
Hope through your blood stream
Half-life flashes of insight.

Breathe in truth.
Simultaneously
Breathe out loss.

Alchemy

The truth

We breathe

When does a poem transform?

Reliving to enlivening

Trauma to healing

Pain to inspiration

Personal to universal

When does a poem transform?

In the writing

In the reading

In the listening

In the existence

Of breathing

Our truth.

About Gabrielle Journey Jones

Gabrielle Journey Jones is a poet, percussionist and event producer born on sovereign Gadigal Land, Sydney, Australia. She is from Maori and African bloodlines and has lived on the Far South Coast NSW, Yuin Country since 2018 with her family. Gabrielle has shared her poetry at local, national and international events for 30 years. She has three other collections of poetry published by Ginninderra Press - Spoken Medicine (2017); Etymology of Courage (2021) and The Purpose of Truth (2023). Gabrielle is looking forward to launching her spoken word audiobook, performing all four collections, made possible by a Lesbians Incorporated grant in 2024.

Gabrielle facilitated and co-edited with Caren Florance "Material & Ephemeral" (2024) the Ekphrasis: Writing About Art Group anthology by 10 local poets reflecting on the 2024 exhibitions at the South East Centre for Contemporary Art (SECCA) in Bega NSW. Gabrielle is inspired by creative communities which celebrate diversity, activism and inclusion. She has worked collaboratively with over 80 organisations delivering poetry and drumming workshops and performances. Gabrielle is also a Senior Social Worker at NSW Health with the Integrated Violence, Abuse and Neglect Services (IVANS). Contact via https://linktr.ee/gabriellejourney

*Author photo by Robert Knapman,
Tathra NSW Yuin Country*